AuthorHouse™
1663 Liberty Drive
Bloomington, IN 47403
www.authorhouse.com
Phone: 833-262-8899

Because of the dynamic nature of the Internet, any web addresses or links contained in this book may have changed
since publication and may no longer be valid. The views expressed in this work are solely those of the author and do not
necessarily reflect the views of the publisher, and the publisher hereby disclaims any responsibility for them.

Any people depicted in stock imagery provided by Shutterstock are models,
and such images are being used for illustrative purposes only.
Certain stock imagery © Shutterstock.

Cover Art by Jen Milton

This book is printed on acid-free paper.

ISBN: 978-1-6655-3742-1 (sc)
ISBN: 978-1-6655-3741-4 (hc)
ISBN: 978-1-6655-3743-8 (e)

Library of Congress Control Number: 2021918484

Print information available on the last page.

Published by AuthorHouse 01/17/2022

authorHOUSE®

Mia Discovers

ITALY

by Alexandria Pereira

The Mystery of History Series

Book 1 of 4

Dedication

To my grandma - for her constant encouragement, wisdom and love.

"Hey, Grandma, where do I come from?" Mia asked.

"I am so glad you asked, Mia," Grandma replied. "You know that you are part of a family. Your mother is my child, and my mother is your great-grandmother. She had a mother too. These are your ancestors, the people who came before you. Mia, you are part of a family."

"But where do I come from?" Mia asked again. "It is a mystery to me."

"Well, our family is also part of a bigger family," Grandma replied. "All the people who live in our city are part of our city family—our neighbors, the people who work in the stores, the people at your school, even the people that play in our park.

"There are other cities with families who live in them too. Let's take a look!" Grandma said. "This is the City of Venice.

"This is the City of Rome.

"And this is the City of Florence.

All these cities make up an even bigger family.

"We call this even bigger family a country. Our country is called Italy. Italy is shaped like a boot.

It hangs off the end of the continent of Europe.

"Italy has mountains, like Vesuvius. Mount Vesuvius is a volcano that has erupted many times.

"Italy has rivers, like the Tiber River, which runs through Rome. Many people like to walk along the river eating ice cream, called gelato.

"Italy has big lakes like Lake Como. Many people like to sail boats on the lake.

"Italy has many, many fields and farms. Grapes are grown in fields and farms, like this one, to make grape juice.

"All these people and many more, including you and I, Mia, live in Italy," said Grandma.

"Here I am, today, with my grandmother.

I see how all the cities, mountains, rivers, lakes, fields, farms, and people are part of my bigger family," Mia said. "I come from this big family—the country of Italy. My history is no longer a mystery. Thank you, Grandma."

"You are welcome, Mia."

Education Support Activities

Basic Human Needs
food
shelter
clothing
the need to socialize
the need to solve problems, invent, and be
creative

Practical Life and Sensorial Foundation
Engage children in activities characteristic
of Italy
plant a seed
wash grapes
sweep outside steps or walkway
hang cloths on a clothes line

History
past, present, and future
timelines

Science
innovation
building and engineering

Geography and Map Work
continents
Europe
significant landforms

Botany
focus on grapes and other agricultural
products of Italy

Earth Science
volcanoes

Peace Curriculum
peace table process
conflict resolution skills

Major Cities, Mountains, Volcanos, Rivers, and Lakes in Italy

Major Cities

Rome	Genoa	Verona	Brescia
Milan	Bologna	Venezia (Venice)	Parma
Naples	Florence	Messina	Taranto
Turin	Bari	Padua	Prato
Palermo	Catania	Trieste	Modena

Mountains
- Mont Blanc, Lyskamm, Matterhorn, and Dent d'Herens are all located in the Pennine Alps on the border between Italy and Switzerland.
- Gran Paradiso is located in the Graian Alps in North Italy.
- La Spedla is located south of Piz Bernina on the border with Switzerland.

Volcanos
- Mount Etna is on the east coast of the island of Sicily.
- Mount Stromboli is on one of the Aeolian Islands north of Sicily, and the whole island is the volcano.
- Mount Vesuvius is located on the Bay of Naples, just east of the city of Naples.

Rivers
- The Po is located in northern Italy.
- The Adige is located in northeastern Italy.
- The Piave is located in northern Italy.
- The Tiber runs through Rome.
- The Arno runs through Florence.

Lakes
- Lake Garda is located in northern Italy.
- Lake Maggiore is located just south of the border with Switzerland.
- Lake Como is located just north of the city of Milan.
- Lake Trasimeno is located south of the city of Florence.

Regions of Italy

Printed in the United States
by Baker & Taylor Publisher Services